shattered sonnets love cards
and other off and back handed importunities

also by olena kalytiak davis

The Poem She Didn't Write and Other Poems
On the Kitchen Table from Which Everything Has Been Hastily Removed
And Her Soul out of Nothing

shattered sonnets
love cards and other off and
back handed importunities

olena kalytiak davis

COPPER CANYON PRESS
PORT TOWNSEND, WASHINGTON

Cover art: Marissa Moore, *16 ways to attach yourself to another human*

Copper Canyon Press gratefully acknowledges Tin House / Bloomsbury
for their original publication of this book.

Copper Canyon Press is in residence at Fort Worden State Park in Port
Townsend, Washington, under the auspices of Centrum. Centrum is a
gathering place for artists and creative thinkers from around the world,
students of all ages and backgrounds, and audiences seeking extraordi-
nary cultural enrichment.

LIBRARY OF CONGRESS CATALOGING-IN-PUBLICATION DATA

Davis, Olena Kalytiak.
[Poems. Selections]
Shattered sonnets love cards and other off and back handed
importunities / Olena Kalytiak Davis.
pages cm
ISBN 978-1-55659-440-3 (paperback)
I. Title.

PS3554.A93757A6 2014
811'.54—dc23

2014026072

98765432 FIRST PRINTING

Copper Canyon Press
Post Office Box 271
Port Townsend, Washington 98368
www.coppercanyonpress.org

acknowledgments

the following poems originally appeared in the following journals:

Agni: "a small number"

The Antioch Review: "six apologies, lord"

can we have our ball back?: "a dry death," "this is the kind of poem i'm done writing, or, *a small pang in spring*," "o great slacker"

The Canary: "keep some stuff for yourself," "aloft in a tangerine cloud"

Conduit: "moorings far faster," "notes toward the ablation of the soul"

FENCE: "poem for my #*th birthday," "she (as sonnet)"

Harvard Review: "a new philosophy of composition, or, how to ignore the non-reasoning creature capable of *speeech* perched outside your bathroom window," "dis-spelt"

LIT: "to dante and cavalcanti and you," "il penseroso and l'allegro: inverted and dubbed," "quain"

The Paris Review: "sweet reader, flanneled and tulled," "small quilled poem with no taste for spring"

Ploughshares: "the unbosoming"

Post Road: "the lais of long lost days," "stripped from the waist up, love"

Tin House: "the true repertory of the wrack and redemption of sir olena kalytiak davis," "you art a scholar horatio, speak to it," "poem convincing you to leave your wife," "to love"

Western Humanities Review: "if you are asked"
Verse: "dear abiah," "in the clear long after," "may be you are like me: scared and awake"

"six apologies, lord" was reprinted in *Best American Poetry 2000* and *The Pushcart Prize XXV: Best of the Small Presses 2001*.

"sweet reader, flanneled and tulled" was reprinted in *Best American Poetry 2001* and *The New American Poets: A Bread Loaf Anthology*, in which also appeared "a small number," "in the clear long after," and "a new philosophy of composition, or, how to ignore the non-reasoning creature capable of *speeech* perched outside your bathroom window."

thanks askold, david, andrew, heather, michael, jim, rob (!) . . . and to all the other kind blind editors.

i am indebted (should be indentured) to the macdowell colony, thank you for my house in the woods full (yet lovely empty) of doppelgängers and fire.

avgustyn! olyana!

and, finally, jim.

dedication

they thought it queer i didn't rise
i thought a lie would be queerer

e.d.

table of dis- mal- contents

forgoodisthelifeendingfaithandfitfully

shattered sonnets love cards
and other off and back handed importunities

sweet reader, flanneled and tulled

Reader unmov'd and Reader unshaken, Reader unseduc'd
and unterrified, through the long-loud and the sweet-still
I creep toward you. Toward you, I thistle and I climb.

I crawl, Reader, servile and cervine, through this blank
season, counting—I sleep and I sleep. I sleep,
Reader, toward you, loud as a cloud and deaf, Reader, deaf

as a leaf. Reader: *Why don't you turn*
pale? and, *Why don't you tremble?* Jaded, staid
Reader, You—who can read this and not even

flinch. Bare-faced, flint-hearted, recoilless
Reader, dare you—Rare Reader, listen
and be convinced: Soon, Reader,

soon you will leave me, for an italian mistress:
for her dark hair, and her moon-lit
teeth. For her leopardi and her cavalcanti,

for her lips and clavicles; for what you want
to eat, eat, eat. Art-lover, rector, docent!
Do I smile? I, too, once had a brash artless

feeder: his eye set firm on my slackening
sky. He was true! He was thief! In the celestial sense
he provided some, some, some

(much-needed) relief. Reader much-slept with, and Reader I
    will die
without touching, You, Reader, You: mr. small-
weed, mr. broad-cloth, mr. long-dark-day. And the italian
    mis-

fortune you will heave me for, for
her dark hair and her moonlit-teeth. You will love her well in-
to three-or-four cities, and then, you will slowly

sink. Reader, I will never forgive you, but not, poor
cock-sure Reader, not, for what you think. O, Reader
Sweet! and Reader Strange! Reader Deaf and Reader

Dear, I understand youyourself may be hard-
pressed to bare this small and un-necessary burden
having only just recently gotten over the clean clean heart-

break of spring. And I, Reader, I am but the daughter
of a tinker. I am not above the use of bucktail spinners,
white grubs, minnow tails. Reader, worms

and sinkers. Thisandthese curtail me
to be brief: Reader, our sex gone
to wildweather. YesReaderYes—that feels much-much

better. (And my new Reader will come to me empty-
handed, with a countenance that roses, lavenders, and cakes.
And my new Reader will be only mildly disappointed.

My new Reader can wait, can wait, can wait.) Light-
minded, snow-blind, nervous, Reader, Reader, troubled,
    Reader,
what'd ye lack? Importunate, unfortunate, Reader:

You are cold. You are sick. You are silly.
Forgive me, kind Reader, forgive me, I had not intended to
    step this quickly this far
back. Reader, we had a quiet wedding: he&I, theparson

&theclerk. Would I could, stead-fast, gracilefacile Reader! Last,
good Reader, tarry with me, jessa-mine Reader. Dar-
(jee)ling, bide! Bide, Reader, tired, and stay, stay, stray Reader,

true. *R.: I had been secretly hoping this would turn into a love
poem.* Disconsolate. Illiterate. Reader,
I have cleared this space for you, for you, for you.

the sonnets

small quilled poem with no taste for spring

In spring all the poems that need to be written
Have. You are neither dejected nor relieved. Scrape and
Paint. Scrape and paint a grey house white.
Feel something! Your husband, the one married to all the
     appetites,
Shouts to someone up on a ladder, someone who looks sort of
Like you: disinterested, spated, thin as a cloud.
It's spring again and so the melancholiacs. And so the fat
Sharp animals pace your roof at night: feeding, quilled,
     recurrent
Dreams. You will never live up to this
Life, they will never refer to you as voluptuous.
You can't remember the last time
you wore a dress.   You pressed your mouth
To the phone.

may be you are like me: scared and awake

A wreath of violets lain where my brain used to be.
  Matutinal,
frantic. The usual. Scalded and cold. I descend. I work like a
  bird.
I hear spring coming from a long mile off. A distant jungle-
  meadow.
It comes, it sings. Says: To be heard you must be let, be in. To
  be heard
It is best to hum, like water. It's true, I am barnacled and
  black. The un-
Derbelly, the sternum, the prow.

                    Was, I used to confess the nuns.
Was, the prettier they were the less they said. Week after week
  whispered
The one I loved like a secret: "I must avow. I'm of that type
  that's mostly
Hype." I let Him forgive her merely on the strength of her
  brow. Sister,
Says I, wear it like a wife. Then I'd go wash my hands in mint
  and rose.
May be, you are like me: all pose.

                    May be, you are cutting each word harder
And harder, to listen. I'm all *watchandwile,waitingtobe Called.*
  Lordy-lordy-lord,

When I asked to be left alone, I didn't mean, like, now, like, this. Full-deep:

All solace and solecism. Un-sail-able. Un-vale-able. To spring, to light, to sleep.

in the clear long after

Spring is cheap, but clean of sky. Long after she used to
meet him on the sly. He didn't say much, because to
speak you need a voice, need lead. Among the dead there were
such fresh ghosts, they were still breathing. Through their
mouths. Time, time, to adjust to an other. An ether
O so—No—too sweet. Intox-icated with permeability. 'Tis nox-
ious, to eat evanescence. However steadily, however slowly.
They stemmed into heady blows.
They missed
the stain. Of blue berries and argument. They missed
their lips. The yew and the thorns. They missed.
Their flaws.

O, to be stung by an errant bee. O, to sting.
O, to see you again. Covered in spring.

march licked me with all his brown lack

as if
someone just handed me
a bouquet
made solely,
entirely,
of the absence
of the word:
Abundance.
Thereby hand-
ing me
everything!

O, to Lack!

I too am made
(mostwholey) of that.

shattered sonnet #3

Love brought
        me a handful
of pussy willows to place
near my face. A sick head
and a sick heart ought be licked
back to health, said said Love,
all stealth. All stick and cue. Love,
didn't I tell you, not to foot
over threshold of mine? But
Love was over, Love was under.
Love was in. Love was wrought.
Love swept the house, then, Love was
done. Aye, There's the rub!
The phoenix and the turtle
dove? Ha! Love, Love is
           nought.

dear abiah

'Tis true,
        we are all made of root
And rue; head-down and head-long, trailing
Like the arbutus.
           O great Arbiter! I keep
A terrible secret. The staves acre. And the back
Ache. And the Longing,
             long and low.

Old, hard news, Desire. That prick! And that
Sting. All but made. All the promises
I intend. To make. To keep. To bend.

               So-long So-sweet! I will
Miss you! Doubt not, or do. I was true. I am
Plaintive, but pliant. Think-me-not
Heart-less or heed-less. None the less: I will.
Ease back. Once again. Yes. Exactly. As does
                   Spring.

a small number

So far, have managed, Not
Much. So far, a few fractures, a few factions, a Few
Friends. So far, a husband, a husbandry, Nothing
Too complex, so far, followed the Simple
Instructions. Read them twice. So far, memorized three
   Moments,
Buried a couple deaths, those turning faces. So far, two or
   Three
Sonnets. So far, some berrigan and Some
Keats. So far, a scanty list. So far, a dark wood. So far, Anti-
Thesis and then, maybe, a little thesis. So far, a small Number
Of emily's letters. So far, tim not dead. So far, Matt
Not dead. So far, jim. So far, Love
And love, not so far. Not so love. So far, no-Hope.
So far, all face. So far, scrapped and scraped, but Not
With grace. So far, not Very.

the lais of lost long days . . .

Today I used my new little hummingbird of a poem to get a
  big old hummingbird of
A bug out the only open, able, window. All my poems are
  hummingbirds, are windows,
Are poems, mostly painted shut. Mostly, suffocate and smile.
  But, hey, I know a good
Simile when I trap it, under glass. *Like a cup. Discarded. Sordid.*
  YOU COULD
NOT. The visitors come from all over to see how I can attend
  to so little for so long. So
Long so sweet! I said that in one of my latest poems. (One of
  my last.) I have finally got-
Ten permission to repeat myself! Myself, never was one to
  relive the past, but now
I've seen that one clip many many times. *Because your Face*
  would put out
Jesus'. Still enjoy it. *That new Grace.* Still think I'm sitting too far
  back. *Pale. Home-*
Sick. Eye. Still realize it isn't great art. Nothing is. Wire
  sculpture that. I know, I know,
It's been done. As I am sure someone has already lived this
  life, this wife, for me. Poor
Fuck. Sick Fish. Lately, I want, (o!), I wish, all my poems to
  end in, to end with,

Spring. The word, I mean. *AND I, COULD I?* Lately, I head
   steadily for,
Tread slowly toward, Abelard. Froward, I mean. I mean,
   Aberdeen.

**june twenty seven eight nine nineteen sixty seventy ninety
six seven eight**

Some one just got on their bicycle, and is, and is
. . . GONE! The Sun makes his mellow his slow his
high-low-way. I send cigarette and coffee drunk postcards to
. . . EVERYBODY! Joe Joe Joe Joe Joe! How hot are you?
To summer, to summit (to submit) properly is a mighty, is a
    difficult
Task. Jenn! O Floating Friend! Are you still on the ferry to . . .
    BUCK
TOWN? There are new guests in my beds but, no.
No visitors, no visions, Love, O. Dear Mary, Hello. It is 9:47 in
    the long
blonde morning. Good Morning, Fair Warning! Hell-
o. O! Luminous Straggler, (don't you know?) all
my post-its are really addressed to no one,
no one, two, three, four but (YOU . . . DON'T . . .
KNOW) O!!!!!!!!!!!!! I sigh,
I sign, with a somber sobriquet,

yrs, X. O.

wow

in sleep and in sickness
in drought and in doubt
for porous for curious for highly and dangerous-
ly adventurous/experimental/momentous
(let me not to the marriage admit pedants, lice, pedophiles)
in truth and in truth and in other sticky-er tricky-er wile-
ier truths (no, not the truths behind that mountain but of the
  sky
behind that sky)
in sleep and in sickness, once again,
in sleep and in sickness, once again,
in clamsauce and in stealth
(let me)
(not!)
through through through
and for for for for
(Admit it!)
EVER!

do you?
tickbird take?
do you?
swallow?

whole?

six apologies, lord

I Have Loved My Horrible Self, Lord.
I Rose, Lord, And I Rose, Lord, And I,
Dropt. Your Requirements, Lord. 'Spite Your Requirements, Lord,
I Have Loved The Low Voltage Of The Moon, Lord,
Until There Was No Moon Intensity Left, Lord, No Moon
    Intensity Left
For You, Lord. I Have Loved The Frivolous, The Fleeting, The
    Frightful
Clouds. Lord, I Have Loved Clouds! Do Not Forgive Me, Do Not
Forgive Me LordandLover, HarborandMaster,
    GuardianandBread, Do Not.
Hold Me, Lord, O, Hold Me

Accountable, Lord. I Am
Accountable. Lord.

Lord It Over Me,
Lord It Over Me, Lord. Feed Me

Hope, Lord. Feed Me
Hope, Lord, Or Break My Teeth.

Break My Teeth, Sir,

In This My Mouth.

the unbosoming

I have been a day boarder, Lord. I have preferred the table to
   the Bed.
I have proffered, Lord, and I have profited, Lord, but little, but
   not. I was Bored,
Lord, I was heavy, Lord. Heavy bored. Hopeless, Lord,
   hideous, Lord. Sexless.
I was in love, Lord, but not with You. The nine malic moulds,
   Lord.
The butcher, the baker, the under-taker. Lord, I was taken
   under. I Repeat
Myself, Lord. I re-peat myself as the way back, the way back to
   Myself,
Lord. I have trembled. His face, Lord, and Yours. I am
   unlovely, Lord, I Nam
Not precious, Lord. Spy better, Love, and You will see:
   Inamnothing. I have Seen
How lovely, Lord, how lovely You are, Lord, but I refused to
   kneel. I Refuse
To knell Your loveliness. I refuse to kiss. And I refuse to tell. I
   am unwilling, Love.
I am unwell. Unkempt. My hideous loins, Love. My body,
   which is all Wrack
And screw, Love. All slack and crewel. At Your beck and call,
   Love, at His Beck

And call. Crestfallen, Love. Of the fallen breast. Un-clean of
   eye. Loose of Thigh.
Ridiculous, Love. Most serious, Love. Unshod. Unshriven. In
   vain and in Rain,

Love. I Live and I Wire. I Wive, Lord, but I Fathom Not.

of yawl and ketch

I have been on watch. Belowstairs, and, Below
Decks. I have watched Night in her fast, Her Feast! O Bellow
-ing Night! Your dark glow, Your worms, Your past. You-Who
Always approach with deceptive, with rosy Retinue

Of dawn. Of dusk. Like you, I have a smallish Task.
O Night, You Tragedian! You placed such splendid Hall
-ucinations before me. Aft

-er those after hours I Yaw
And I catch, but they, They carry it with them, steadily Abaft:
Their hips, their faces, Their breasts, their Masks.

in one of my lives—

This one—If I must Be—
Exact, all others hid their edges. A Tide
Passed over the long black grass, the sky Grew
Green and bigger, I drank red potions in Satiating
Portions. But—having Nothing—
To compare it to—I Saw
Felt, tasted Nothing.

To Think—
Once I was taught a Foreign
Language with words—like Seeds
Of poppies! Trice I was brought a Bouquet
Of yellow—butterflies, alighting! Unfurling—
And all I could think: I am thrice—unfurling. Next Door
They built a house of Noise. The tiny hammers and Anvils
Inside my ears—never ceasing. Next door: I was Left—
Ajar—having too little to say to my few and Far,
My friends. And you, fair friend—who Stayed
So Long—we had to call It
A big old windy Dwelling.
A three hundred sixty five star Night.
A Day.

In one of my Lives
I didn't know How—

Good—I kept my bird-like arms—Folded
Under what should have Been
My chest what should have Been
My heart—made the Usual
Small—human—Noises.

dis-spelt

Away, away
Now that I have told the man I love
I do not love him, I will need a new, a way.
Now that I have admitted to my dis-
Passion, my dis-possession, my dis-ease.
I will need new ways, new stars, new bones,
New trees. I leave
With me I bring my blue-veined feet,
My jeweled face, my dis-pleasure, my dis-ease.
I pack, unpack my orange streaked,
My freakèd heart. With me I bring
My prosthetic soul. Under the newly dis-astering
Stars I dis-limn, dis-orb, dis-robe. O new dis-aster!
I will need new breasts, new legs, electric shock.
A clock, a clock. I will need to dis-pose of my
dis-pose. My sorry starry pose. Now
dis-arranged, now dis-natured, now dis-
Owned. My dis-comfiture, my dis-comfort,
My dis-content: none dis-edged, none dis-closed.
All tree and bones! Dis-furnished
Among the turning leaves and the burning faces, do hang.
My dis-candied dis-course burnished, banished
Dis-patched abroad. Dis-lodged, dis-mayed, dis-
Played like this, like these,

Like sylvia's leaves, like dead letters sent
To dear(est) him that lives alas! away
Now that I have, now that I have
Alway, alway.

quain

having hoisted my stay sail here I linger
in this my well my heavily an notated
sick ness having stay ed staid staying here I
so journ in this wind blown chat eau this full
blown season here I carefully craft
my moon hump am told am un am folded by
the bitter berried winter nauseated
by noon and enervated by eve
whether by fort night or by twelve month
o season o chateau dish abille after
hours and dis habille after noon here here
I wait I wait and most ly here I slow ly
winter smoke able thick as a snow cloud
dawn sick and sick to death of dusk

to dante and cavalcanti and you

was on the road of sighs once
once was my traveling habit simple
a riding dress black my heart
my heart from whence it came hence

I went came out small fallible foiled shook
aflame (andmostlytoblame) (andmostly) fallen
short withnot an ounce or pint to spare
said (said) (said) was out on a dare was o lovely-asunder!

let came to half-lit awash in a low and lonely light
to a long in the field with him to live or die
love with a horsepond but (alas) no (notsofast) horses

end it with a send up: vanna and bice and me
send our delicately scented innards our o so small
regard(s) not quite yrs love(')(s) b g o

she (as sonnet)

I had

been thinking about leaving the house for a while now; simply
    walking into that

huge japanese screen set infront of it like a city. But the thinner you
    are the heavier she

gets: I was so weighed down: anchor-hearted, lead-souled. I had
    resolved not to speak

to her; to avoid all pathetic fallacy when it came to her, but she was
    everywhere

(verywhere): the skeletal houses where her, the ladders were her,
    the abandoned cars.

Boxes, birds, she even lived on paper. A paperthin sheet, she was
    an onion and an

orange, she was a mountainside, she was that one red cloud: oh
    luminous straggler!

She consumed all my thought, she made it hard to answer the
    phone, to write a fine let-

ter. She got in the way, between me and what I was meant to do on
    these backlit

winter days. The sun and the moon and the seas, the sea: she
    swam there as well.

She arrived in the mail.
She was the scratch in every mirror.

She, the one with bare shoulders, the one that I love love loved.

letters to various personages

**the true repertory of the wrack and redemption
of sir olena kalytiak davis**

remember not, spied no
light, upon the molehill je m'appelled
detroit. someone drove me off a cliff,
in skiff with wheels and lungs. word was world laid
upon whorled, ear heard, but h(ear)t couldn't
tell, didn't know above
from, let alone, below.
bellowed long and low. already it wounded
and it pinked, but i dare not call it
SOUL. i dare not call it "i."

was immunized, was shot,
against the sicknesses of the heart and lot,
of the sordid sort (of the dawn
and of the dusk, of the wake and of the boat), but didn't
comport, stung but didn't stick. i,
poor "i," got sick.

was am was small and despisèd
tall in my anger in my thrust and stall
and all and always was pretty was much
a wreck from the neck
down hung low stayed staid but left, left, got right
out of town

on the transport called love
(but it was nothing of the sort)
(it was neither train nor port).

the first was a boy with a (volley) ball
he wrote me a (love) letter or two
i kissed him in a (ski) jacket
but he didn't recognize me in june.

then richboy, punkrocker, prufrock, short
order(andunder)cook(ed), thief! a drummer all
summer, then
an old(er) man-
imal that liked to eat
his young

then you (but who are is you am i talking to?)

no, i know:

was my was first was real was love
hard on a park bench and long and low
(and long)
(and hard)
but somehow moved to what was it (?) what was
it (allowed) (to be) looked out upon:

o heavenly earthly pulchritude!
o man,
and, fuck, o wife.

a solitary a field
east-west of here, and fickle,
only when wet

with beginning rain, or lit
with early evening snow.

then a different meadow opened
and i, poor i, bent over, got on knees, cupped hands, drank
drank from the stream

let out the scream (the scream the scream)
(o love i am so different)

went from mr. longlove (you *were* my patient log man)
to master wronglove (and back) and back (and back)
but couldn't get the knack couldn't get
in groove in grove in glove in tongue in hat
couldn't tell which from what
who day night from rat

heart spoke heart broke
but what the fuck is that?????

heart has only silly things to do to say.
the heart is an ear.
a wig. and, yes, yes, a fist. the heart is

no bigger than that. than this.

started shoveling shoved (snow) shoed hard,
showed you this, was feigned was am (not?), i think, remiss,
   remiss,
got nowhere, i.e.

here
this

head hurt
heart hurt
skirt didn't fit,

asked to be quickened
(to say to the passing stay)
but was misunderstood
by some god (or his underling)

(skort didn't fort a thing)

birthed two babes on top of it
(o i labored in the stubble field . . .)
(each sex a flower stranger than the last . . .)
((always) already told you that) (you this)

was unglued was undone
a small and heavy flower
all head became all stem
lost went at a head
was once became stronger
than the rest (but you but i but you was were are am not
     impressed)

impressed?
press here, press this,
(now, now!)

now (as in so much to be done 'tween now, 'twixt now
and six and six and six)

now
it is

now.

how?

work done love here
and gone and look at me:

all flesh and fold: all shelter
from the fucking storm (the snow falls, love)
(love, but it doesn't stick)
this was this not this foretold
(they heal me with their little hands)

and *joy is what i like, that,*
and love. (and love.)

forgoodisthelifeendingfitandfaithfully

and *grief absent joy is present*
for that time

but look, look, look
here here now now
at me at me, at this:

i said look at me.
all right. all ready. (alright, already!)
look:

nothing left
to the imagination.

dear beardtongue

o, how long it's been
since i put soul
to lips (or, for that matter,

lips to soul!) (swallowing sound) (effect)

once i was thick with it,
but eros sickened
went

after being vaulted and vaunted
someone defaulted
(but i don't think it was i)
(for as they say: *i was not i*)

now, here, without the seasons
i find i am found (but lost, but lost)
(at half the cost)

the shift i wear i wear well
no longer weary-worn or -torn
by ether-things by other-things

by ground i am ground
by (t)reason shorn

i mostly sit and walk
on dirt. alone. nothing
has grown in me,
(save child after flowering

child) (each sex a stranger flower
than the last) but i remain
unblown

for i have not wintered
in years now
so how (now) how then
spring? (or even fall?)

if i could miss you
i would with all my mouth
(all month long)

if i could kiss you?
torn.

for i find myself
minding my
earthlythings,

for i am newly made of flesh
newly flesh-bound
and bo(u)rn(e)

yours, love, o.

letter home

dearest(s)! and dearer still! and still more dear!
was afloat in the sea of the sky
(wondered why why why?)
but now i dare now i know now i see
through clouds of snow

greetings from my bubblebath
well, by that i mean my this, my day
whenever i say "bathtub" read "day"
read away!
whenever i say "poem,"
which i won't, read "stay"

the bubbles rise and float,
come to a head, lodge in my throat

yes, there are things i must still
requite and things that are all right and those must stay
unrequited   still
you you you are the only thing
the only thing
that i have not done, not right

(*i was born to be lonely,
i am best so*) (ho ho ho)

mr. solitary, my new lover,
he has just washed my hair
with a certain degree of flair

and already there is talk of betrayed
upon betrayal (out on an outback trail)
(like i said, loves, instead of "love" read "fog"
instead of "poem" use "delay")
love leans against
against my window case
creaks like a tall tree, like a wreck

hey, why do we always fall in love with a fairy or a nymph?
(or something like that) (an imp! an imp!) (but, come on, a
   blip? a blurb? a blimp?)

mine is was blue with a pinched nose and a spreckled face
a mr. twisty shirt
imagine, a fate like that like this

like this like that in no time flat
the woods have transplanted themselves
outside my mullioned window   splat
and this morning it quaked me awake
to make me feel right and right

at home, o dears, i wrote you a pome!
(a long letter home!)

in one of the panels floats you

and you

and you

(one multiplied by three, if you count
the other one, two)

my little bees
i see i see (i see!)

while i am gone, please

raise my children up from the plain ground
your elves, my pucks and my sprites,
lest they go away to college
(to collage!) lickety split(e)

make sure they say their prayers
to the pale moon and the sleepless sky

lest their mother
one day die

and so far, so far!,
my magic, my book
i have not drowned
have lit my spleef
here, all bathtub long,

heard talk of having made a building sing
(all the women come with singular visions,
all the men just look at to me)

(art art here i art! but with
out an eye with   out
gloves a heart)

loves, i am no longer suicidal!
i drove my bike into the short strangled night
was lit by it

by conduct of some star
(mis- of mine (nay, don't say, of your?) own)
i made make my way

some star, three

the outlook is
bubbly is foggy
i long to write and right my wrong
to kiss you drunk and kiss you stoned

and stoned
the outlook
out back
is (i'm coming!) (back!)
(no longer called!)
up up up
and away

poem convincing you to leave your wife

hey you, you
of unbuttoned flannel
shirt and untold charm,
if you hear heard that rauschenberg
has had painted a new painting, the wisest
thing to do would be to drop
everything you are
doing and manage
one way or another to see
it. no?

have you dare you see seen it?

(as i was going to st. ives, i met a man with seven wives
every wife had seven faults
every fault had seven bolts
every bolt had seven tries

bolts, faults, tries, wives,
how many were going to st. ives?)

duck is duck. and
fuck is, i'm afraid, fuck. it's you that i miss, that i want.
i espouse that you come here and miss me too.
now.
now, as is: *how much to do 'tween now and six.*

where o where on this moonlit and dreamvisited planet are
    you?
are you willing? are you well? are you sick? *(i'm sick of love,*
    nar, nar)

this is just to say:
lover, it's over. and
it's not.

o lizzie dearest (here's letter within letter): i have met with
    your old flame
and became unsettled
about imemine. mien.

meow.
who is to blame?

he thinks of you monthly
and would like to meet and fuck biannually
he has had a vasectomy
and sex with other men.

are you game?

funny, what we harbor when we do. and where. and how.
   (how long) (how low)
(below, below.)

but, an excellent driver stoned!

i have decided that we do not want other people's (wives')
   husbands
as we do not want our own.

as we do not want our own.

(i cannot live with you becuz
that would be
IZ life!)

o liz
twixt impunity and impurity
lie i
and lies my art

so, i will do as i am told:

love your neighbor as yourself
and put your cup up on your shelf

ask the kindly sexton for some kinky sex
on the slide and on the sly on the fence
(if you're brave enough to try)

FOR (listen up!) *no concrete test of what is really true has ever been*
agreed upon.

FOR SOME *make the criterion external to the moment of perception,*
putting it either in revelation,
the consensus gentium,
the instinct of the heart (aye! there's the rub)
or the systematized experience of the race (three men in a tub)

OTHERS *make the perceptive moment its own test:*
use common sense (à la reid)
use synthetic judgment a priori (kant not cunt)
the inconceivability of the opposite (but i was never into that)
the capacity to be verified by sense (now, now, now that!)
the possession of complete organic unity
or self-relation (realized when a thing is its own other)

o brother!
i long to be realized like that!

back to "you," will you come and realize
me? would you could
you?
be my other? now and for a short time.
like b'twixt six and nine,
nine and six.

we may have acquired it by fair means or by foul;
passion may have whispered it
or accident suggested it; but if the total drift
of thinking continues to confirm it, that is
what s(h)(w)e mean(s) by true.

i renamed it and it remained and i remain, yours,
the wife that st(r)ayed and the wife that left(ed), o.

skirts traps wraps thighs . . .

we had stayed up all night, my friends and i

singsaying:

LEAVE DADA
LEAVE YOUR HUSBAND
LEAVE YOUR WIFE

(BUT AUGIE, NOT YOU
DO NOT EVER LEAVE YOUR
DEAR OLD TWISTED MAMA)

for if we leave

it as is
(for) now (for) ever
you will remain cult
and i, poor i, lost cunt.
yours, love, o.
yours so.

o to make the air turn glue and rubber!

science says "what exists" (it's like a list)
but, to compare the worths
both of what exists and what does not
(what thou wast and what thou art)
we must consult not science
but what pascal calls (ya) our (le) (lay) (mine) (m'old lazy)
heart

*(le coeur a ses raisons que la raison
ne connaît pas)* (shut up!)

my heart is cool
and black

is fool and blank

nevertheless
nevertheless

i remain,
the wife that staid and the wife that left
the wife that laughed and
the wife that slayed

riffs miffs thoughts knives . . .

what exists and
what, alas, does not

what i wast
and what i art

not

word is and
word was (unheard
of!) rauschenberg has painted
a new painting. i dare not
(meet me there)
go!

keep some stuff for yourself

i have never told anybody
about the time i i i
slept with three guys at once

cause it never happened

but why o why
did i say anything about
the ping–pong table, the slits
that were his eyes, the river that now runs
backwards, and about the o! o! o!
meadow?

how it was
crossed and recrossed
and crossed

out the grass turning to sea
to wallow

how i crossed my heart and hoped
to finally and decisively

live but died o,
so young and so hard, killed

everything
was resurrected
into somebody's mother, somebody's (x?) wife

did i mention my first kiss was extracted
by someone who never should have been that
lucky? and how much later i threw
my virginity and, later still, my vanity
away?

probably

how now i'm wearing them again, like a strapless
backless dress and a powerpuffs backpack?
like a pinkblueyellow hand knit woolen cap?

i have not told anyone, but,
like marty running, i too have shat my pants

remember that navy blue night when your friend's wife told
your husband in the dark
among the dripping roses
that you were trying to steal
hers?

and you didn't know it then
but yours was already lost
and gone?

actually, i probably have already said
a word or two about that
to one or two

and do you recall when X called you unamunam-
unambitious?

you told many many many tales about that
except that maybe you are, were

when will you learn to keep it
quiet
for god's sake

don't tell anyone
you sent your son flying
into a jamb, it was a door he was up against,
it was this hard as a board this life
his my eye
and the blood in it, for you

excuse me,
i have laid aside or betrayed

every one and thing you have ever . . .
owed
owned
sown
thrown
wanted
got

sometimes do you have to step outside your life
or, at least, outside your house, when it was (nay, is) late late
late at night to see how bright
and warm where you live is, was
how right?

and even then you didn't and don't believe it
because you are and are not right
is was and is wasn't
and it ain't

wrong or right

i have yet to say much of anything on the topic
of being the betrayed instead of the betrayer

of what was left
on my husband's cell

like *in the bedroom* like *unfaithful*
i, (you too?), have disposed of the body

singing: *honesty*

is a luxury

will you spare me

the gory details:

okay, so you yourself have fucked with your eyes your hand
    your cunt
closed over somebody else's cock

and turns out they were really fucking "you"

sometimes
bite out your his our her lovely tongue(s)

mind the tip of your nose, where your fingers went, how you
  got down
on your knees, look out
for your pink your black
your steel colored and cloud covered . . .

go ahead, sell that stupid old soul, but, please, mind your step,
  your mind. please
please,
pletase!

keep some of it
some of this (shhhhhhhhh . . .)
some of . . . iiiiiittttt
for yourself

to love

love,
i am expecting

you
always

love, for you
i am always

wearing
never weary

whether
with my hair
tied back or hanging

down
my deepest cut
shirt

my lowest slung
pants

love,
my waist

love,
when i am tired
when i expire

i am will be
thinking of you
walking in

love, you

at the end of every
long short journey

at the end of every drive
way i expect

love,

you would joy
and moan

to see what
my face does
for you

daily

how it opens each
day how it lies

at night

for you
in wait

other importunities

**a new philosophy of composition, or, how to ignore the
non-reasoning creature capable of *speeech* perched outside your
bathroom window**

It was bleak december just last night or the night
just before ~ *Pravda!* I mean, *It's true!* ~ like Prado says: god
had taken poetry away from you: a stone
was just a stone. But today today today everything
is pinioned, laced, and fuck me!, new: this crazy purple
toothbrush afloat in the complicated trash, that
strange yellow bird over there, and the blue-green sash
that hangs in the rosepale sky speaks to you ~ o.k., o.k.,
I mean, to me: each word, like, say, cor-bi-ere and la-for-
gue means something more than it used to ~ did, did! gather
gather gather and round because today I'm made
of sacred ground everything plants itself inside me grows
(I know now what was missing then I know now what was
present then it was moving it was still but I couldn't see
within) now now now it stops and spires, now now now
it rolls and gyres ~ Yeats!: *here all the barrel-hops are knit
here all the serpent-tails are bit here all the gyres converge
in one . . .* I meant: *Yikes!* and, no, I'm not done ~ a fire is
in me head! I'm in the zone!: in Marseilles among the wa-
termelons in Coblentz at the Giant's Hostelry in
Rome under a Japanese medlar tree! Surely, surely
it's the second coming! "*. . . or the third,*" broke in who 'til then
seemed like such a sweet and mellow bird, under his beak, but

I heard him, I heard him . . . What matter! The rhythm
finds me rinds me books open brooks open too I have eur-
asian steps matches tipped-blue that light on anything
everywhere I'm a live a fire a flame in this morning
light I'm far more bright than must be right. I can hear
the defunctive music! I can glean and gleam and brew
today I believe I might be able to do
what was once to me assigned years ago and you're right!
only last last last lastnight! Finally! dickinson's
and modigliani's sex exposed! Finally! I can
see the foreign clocks the feather beds the eider-
down and the long white cocks fish that swim and open letters
to boot sweaters warm again! "The worst are filled with
passionate intensity—" Warned again! by that
unseemly but seemingly well-educated bird
as if on cue, but, hey, I shot right back: take thy beak
from out my heart, said I, 'cause, like, What matter! These
photos once framed now cough and sneeze this pen rights it-
self flows with ease and I can feel the trees remember
their long lost leaves ~ o.k., o.k., so the dogs bark
as they have barked and barked before but the road came by
and drove me out to shore sails set sail and pails fill up with
sand lovers dress set out for land berrigan marries not-
ley again! and again! again my husband dawns a new
hand sown and flowered shirt I weigh much much less today and

more and more I float above the moat full of serpents beasts
and other fiendly things the castle sways the horses take
on wings ". . . *And Philomel becometh dumb*" ~ but O! not you
bleak-beak-ed burd-en ~ o.k., o.k., Quoth I: *What-ever!*
Who cares if you laugh as you have laughed and laughed
    before,
behind my back when I was just a somber bore, a strag-
gler headed east, then west, with a pocket full of seeds
and subway tokens, a cracked tooth, and Damn!, a broken
nail. Bitten, bitter, lit! Forsooth and forsaken! Lo! I
traveled but it wouldn't travel me, I smoked and turned to
graying smoke, I listened to all they had to say ~ felt dick ~
turns out I held it in until today! *Sacré-Coeur!*
Today I am so found I am newly lost. Vallejo!
I mean: *Way-to-go!* What happens next happens now! Today
I have drunk the stone and I will carry it with me, for
a short long luminous while.

you art a scholar, horatio, speak to it

You say you walk and sew alone?
I walk and sew alone.

You say you gape and waver?
I am mostly dizzy, most open-mouthed.

You say you taste it with each dish?
I drink it and I spit it up.

You say it lays you face-down?
I kiss the dirt.

Carved into your bone china?
Mine's more fine.

Folded into your laundry?
Dry. Dry. Dry.

Is it quite awful and unbearable?
Quite.

Is it sweet and gentle?
Most sweet, most gentle.

Does it make you retch?
I am wretched.

Do you write it poems?
I compose on it daily.

Is it epic?
In thought and in treatment.

Do you cry upon it?
It is flat and wet.

Will you humor it?
Forever.

Will you forsake it?
Never.

You say you keep it in a box?
I've Cornelled mine.

You say you call it soft names?
I call it softly. I name it.

Clipped of fledge?
Clipped of fledge.

You say it sits up on your soul?
It has it licked.

A new religion?
Nay, a faith.

Do you take it to bed?
I've pillowed and I've laid with it.

Does it propagate?
I sharpen my chastity upon it.

I belt it. I go down on it.
I keep it down.

Have you done your best to bury it?
I have dug.

With half a heart?
With dull spade, yea, half-heartedly.

Has it a sword?
A long-tailed lion on its crest.

Would you unknow it?
I've called it bastard.

Bastard!
Would you divorce it?

Untie it, would you?
Have you

Done with it?
No. I will have more.

moorings far faster

what did your lover promise behind the lids of her eyes what
    music
a place where a charge for

it doesn't matter that it's not your name
what matters is that it calls you what matters is out there

somebody yearns for you tongues your name and then
she referred to them as lovers as if they handled love

with their bare hands wet slo-pitched gloveless tongue
in groove a love lit and lowered it glowered

and it wormed some body else's lover called me this
    morning
his voice heavy with it but me *i don't touch the mud*

so what shall i do with your knocking *it is you that i love*
it is you that i love

and what shall i do with what you whispered
in both ears *so much so much*

and that one mooring you lifting a worm-girl out
of a boat out past the waves out past her own small fragile

body and then your name or your not-name
but spoken as you've never heard it spoken

before they have never loved you
the way you wanted to be loved they have never lifted you

above the water how small whatyouareaskingfor and how
   large
their denial yourfatheryourbrotheryourwormyourwife

despite ominous forebodings of sin sickness and death

The red shirt you wear in the underworld of my dreams is a
thick bright shade.

Oh, the aniseeds: it's alright, you can swallow them. And i
looked it up, you are allowed to dream smells! Ginger,
nutmeg, a certain well-known pungent herb, and yes, even
gorse. Yes, yes, obviously, you will be surrounded by fields
and fields of poppies. Black pods will be stuck in the seams
of your teeth.

Do not despair.

This means you are lucky.

Although you are not allowed to wait for me in front of certain
small bookstores; although you are not allowed to run into
me on the entirely wrong corners of certain
long
entirely wrong
streets,
if you find yourself

in my hereafter (do not be alarmed) attired in red shirt, black
leather vest. Rest assured, this has nothing to do with
personal style, metaphysics, nor, even, syntax: Do not
despair.

It means: "You are lucky."

il penseroso and l'allegro: inverted and dubbed

Hence sordid bullshit, leave me the fuck alone,
with my milton and my dickinson
with my browning and my keats
with my quillless pen and my yeats—nothing
rhymes anymore, yet it is possible to master
to make it neat, when allroundyou is the disaster
of soul on soul gone bad, rotten or rotting
from the edges on in. Let me suffer
friendless and forlorn, let me toil and toll
that bell for me alone, I don't need any
charity. I only need and empty space to rest in.

Hence seriousness and melancholy
who couldn't use a little late in the millennium folly
at this latedateandtime—I've been furrowing my brow
too long now, I need a little rap a little weed any song
to relieve me of this form this world where men just fucking sit
    and moan
admit you are insignificant (magnificent) and all alone
and move on, young man, cause you're a drag
to be around, despite your quaint acerbic wit, you lag
behind the times, go pump someiron or somecunt,
there is still honey to be tasted, and look at you, you've
    already wasted

a lot (two words) of your heavenly earthly time. I'll not waste
  mine.
I'll yet learn to (fuck and) sing.

poem for my #*th birthday

today, in honor of my #*th birthday,
i put on my new pink low rise corduroy
flares

today, in honor of my #*th birthday,
augie and lyana (my winnowed minnows) swam synchronized
naps

today, in honor of my #*th birthday,
i changed the sheets on my bed from baby blue to red to red
to red . . .

today, in honor of my #*th birth,
i watched #*# w**dru^^, who i slept with once or twice (in
    1986), report from islamabad
for abc

(he still looked good!) i would sleep with him again, today

in honor of my #*th birthday, i brewed up just for me
a whole pot of prince vladimir tea, i mean,
thé

today, in honor of my 3*th,
i remembered berrigan's birthday poem and *his* birthday pants
(i think he was turning burning twenty seven eight nine
ten!)

and the new york sky, returned to his sky

and his heart, and frank's, and, given many more years and tries,
(but, now, that's not how it works, is it?) maybe
mine!

today, in honor of my birth, my rebirth, i was frank and i was
    ted
(i was (would have been) that good in bed) but my husband
    was nowhere to be
found

he was let loose he was hunting moose
near magrath on a
raft

(a fat new moose of a lover in his boney head)

and remember, there were also those nasty birthday poems by
  sylvia by sylvia
plath plath plath? and šalamun wrote a wonderful little
  birthday poem, with that army
shit and *tommy* in it,

and who else? i don't know.
i'm secretly not that well read,
although it's a secret i keep only from
me

(from me, from me)

today, in honor, to preserve my honor, my poetic honor, my
  code,
i actually went and found that little black book with the lace
  appliqué,
that book i stole from the juneau public librar(and it was/is
  rare)y

following in ted's boots, his foots, his falls, his steps . . . *(still to
  do today: smoke more*
cigarettes, steal some books . . .)

and my god! look! berrigan also had a birthday shirt! dear old
     (and he was so young) ted was
always over over over
over the fucking top, good for fucking
him

today in my honor,
thought: at the top, am i, of my game

today today today, in honor of my thirty and my eight,
i ate i ate i ate
i decided to stay up late late late

i celebrated
i berated (almost) no one (and it was already after
noon)

but i never should have picked at, picked up that cake, i mean
     (and i *am* mean)
that cate or that spenser

i mean, short
i mean, too long
too young
too dean, i mean,
too earnest
too important
too marvelous
too much
and
not not not not near or far enough

is one day
to celebrate
my miraculous, my moment
-ary, my airy, my aerie, my moment
of inertia, of truth
my
-ous, and my
-tum, my monument of a
birth,
my lovely girlie-girth!
no maid am i, but still not bad, not bad . . .

today, in honor of my 38th,
i wrote this poem,
and i haven't written
a poem in years!
in years,
in years . . .

oh my friends, to you, in tears, i drink a beer
your old friend is thirty is thirty is thirty—
eight, right now, today!
though some of you forgot, oh, forget (it) away . . .

what would my long not heard from friend joe have to say
    about all this?
what would my tall short found long lost (friend or foe?) matt
    have to say
about anything at all?

i must go read his new book and find out!

still to do in honor of my birth(to)day:
go for a short-long walk
buy some milk (both skim and whole)
hold off on that pregnancy test until next week when i'm not
    so depressed

not be so depressed!

eat many many many more m&ms (line then up, pair them up,
    by color, by design) by birth

yeah, give kids bath (more bubbles, mama, and less troubles,
    please, say they)

kiss their faces and their bellies, their fingers and their tips

get rid of them, palm them off to sleep, to sleep, to sleep, and
    then,

watch a good movie or

write mary *(mary, have you seen anything good lately?)* or finish
    reading

the good (well, the all right) *soldier*

for god's sake: stop and think!

mastermastermasterbate

sleep my self, my way to not today, to not my (birth)day

yet some how try to always to feel this this

this commemorative this commemorated

finally not under rated or sedated

(look, see here: my fireworks! my flat stomach *and* the fruit of
    my womb! my flares!)

tomorrow, in honor of my birthday: DO NOT REVISE
THIS
poem
this
life
this
everything
and
anything
(is something, ain't it, love?) love?

where? and, when?

tomorrow:
buy birthday shirt: it will (will it?) be red or
orange or pink

not yellow!
not blue!

notes toward the ablation of the soul

The soul should not be multiplied needlessly, i.e.: the dull razor
of your soul. Your straight-
back soul, your slo- pitched
soul, your soul that throws out
largesses on all sides without
counting: Full Beautiful! Full Soon!
Your soul that sounds like a string
quartet: but is really just a violin
and a viola. Your diatonic
soul. Your diacritic soul, your soul that hates
just-about-fucking-everything: id est: the one
with an eye for imperfection, the lungs
of a butterfly. The perfected soul.
The perfect animal that is your soul: wet,
gutted. The guttered soul, caught
out in the rain, your soul in gold lamé, your soul,
the crooner. Your fucked-up singing
soul. Your lame soul. Your flat soul.
The soul that is your body.
That soul.
Her bare shoulders.
The hardening off of the soul. The soul
stiff. The soul with a hard-on. The husbandry
of the soul. Your vegetable soul: eyed-green
and black. Fructified. Addicted

to borage and hell-bore. Your paper soul: the wasps'
nest. Your swarming soul: the invisible bees circling
the rusted mail-box that is your soul and your soul inside it:
mailed and nailed. (Your soul with a past of plank
and slowness.) The cross-eyed soul, the looking glass
of the soul: your odonate soul, its small
sharp teeth. The soul that counts
like a mother. The unmoved
soul and the accompanying soul;
the soul that walks with you
but on the other side of the street. The soul alone
and palely loitering.
The three totalities of the soul. The sidereal soul.
The crystal soul. The empyrean.
Your innermost soul, your in-
land soul, your sea-sick soul. Her cordage.
The restive soul, the ignore-all-the-rest soul.
The soul wrapped in eiderdown.
The seleniferous soul, neither new nor full.
The soul, uncertain. The soul, unwell.
Your soul the sick taper. The tomato
worm. The pleached soul. The bleached soul.
The bleating soul. The bloated soul.
The soul, pleading: there's-no-such-thing-as-a-soul, soul.
The smoking soul. Through her flared nostrils . . .

The snared soul. The bridled soul. The soul's barouche, her
    pied
horses. The piebald soul. The dappled
soul. The soul that selves. The starfish.
The soul that faiths. Yet remains
faithless. The soul that prefers
to decline. Dirndled and kirtled, the queen's
soul: the longspun, the finespun,
the dizzy soul, spun
finer and finer still. The still-
born soul. The soul born snapping her fingers (Šalamun's soul).
The plagiarized soul. The 10th plague, the plague
of the flying souls. The dying soul. The soul standing still.
The standstill of the soul.
The sandfill of the soul. The soul no one asks about.
The soul that recognizes itself
by its coat. Your soul: the train-wreck,
the soup-çon, the tea-cup. That scant and edged.
Your soul, you dare call
that splendid? S: You can stay or go . . .
The sunspots on your soul.
The bare spots of the soul. The stretch and track-
marks. The soul shooting up. The soul shot. The old soul sold
out, the odd soul out, out
having swum beyond its ken,

the damned soul out
finally, out
out out
of your
system.

sign offs

a dry death

prologue

boatswain! must our cunts be cold?
must our hips be hips
for children to sit on?
must this ache be ache-not-nearly-ache-enough?

o, i labored on the stubble plain
(long heath, brown furze),
but baby was born in a field of phlox.

i.

fret not, baby, thy mama was
a piece of virtue. betid,
bootless though she was,
she never did take her boots off!
god clothed her for a reason.
what was was not
meant to be seen.
thus her vanity was her virtue
and by what undid her
she was hid.

maybe she dreamt it.
maybe she tempted
fate more than she did them.

baby, if not a very good one,
it was a way to live.

know, though, you were her he-
and her -art.
and ma-ma-me your sycorax,
(with age and envy grown
into a hoop)
your dam, your she.

anyway, bottom line:
the island's yours.

ii.

her body was a piece of work of
art. the kind that made you feel
challenged after leaving the museum but glad
that youyourself were never that fucked

up. still. it was all sort of scary and reassuring,
that somebody else thought that. that you
could too, but for you it wasn't urgent, you
could go home from it, you
would have to buy the postcard

to really remember it. in detail. well and lit.
it didn't live you. you
were for all intensive care purposes
healthy as a fucking horse. it was she
who was sick. as sick
as a taper, sick as a corpse.

it attracted you, being
repulsed like that. it made you
happy! imagine that! wasn't life
intense? so much was hidden!
imagine, also, that.

iii.

in new york the weather took the t-shirt
right off your back. you
in a summer breeze was more
than i could take.

i would always see shirts that i would hang you in.

i would always see shit that you did and it disappointed me
in some totally fundamental way, that you went on
to live.

i was fatal, was i not?
but, i, i was not i. i was
bent.

iv.

come here, fickle-fingered
fate. come here and take your strap, i mean, cap off.

it was a rat that sat in a hat.
a hyena. i'm no madonna.
but, look: the fucking eland,
the baby weaned

before i was.
we both screamed: it's so unfuckingfair!
but what we both wanted was never there.
(was never there.)

the fairies and the tales. you could pin them down
but you couldn't put them up.
i meant the opposite, apposite was i,
was, i sang and supped.

but what was there is there to describe?
didn't don't we have eyes enough?

v.

and if i seduce you with my thin hips
and lips and lips will you spin will you turn
and burn? and run? or will you sleep and keep it?

yum.

an empty house.

and the mailman feeds the box.

and i brew this up for you

(baby was born in a field of phlox . . .)

and you mix it with your gin
and you take it on your chin
with your mescaline and your X.

(you were always busy sitting on a fucking fence.)

and he who's not buzy bein'
buzzed, born (i labored labored labored) bruised
iz buzy dyin'

and she born to be hanged
need fear no drownin'

(boatswain?)

(o boatswain!)

the bards were are barks, were our barges.
we were their charges, but we missed the fucking boat.

o. no. naught nautical.
sank there, drowned that.

and remind me, who who who
have i did i do i love?

who did i do? and who did i that?

(and what in god's sake did i prove?)

vi.

fuck you.

i wasn't airy on the page, i was fucking ariel
on the page, but when where they said tempest i thought

they said temptress (lie there, my art!)
and i could do it (do you) even without
the golden tressssssssssss, but

believe me, more to know did hiss
did mettle in (was metal in) my thoughts,
but what what what was supposed to hang
there (clang!) there (hang that!) there
were a curtain or a sail
once were? once went?

vii. (epilogue)

a dry death for me.

and daily. our father
who art dead, died sorting spinach, after shovelling off
the drive a light
light snow. o. thekingmyfather'swrrrrrrrrrrrrrrrrrrrack.

SMACK

no, you're right, was i,
i was the one who sorted, snorted,
sordid was. was the light
that died, that lit, that flew.

look at me: a face
like a worn fuckin' sail,
the brow of an ancient
-ship, -pin, -dom, neither king
(nor kitten) nor kind.

my mind a sunken trunk.

my complexion: perfect
gallows.

sign off #1

and then i knew it: i too was one of the falsifiers.
there was no longer the question of ascent or expiation.
i would live slowly, like the rest of them.
i would die unvisited: a small dark cloud in the rosepale sky.

sign off #2

and thus i remain: both illuded and illumed.
having not quite quit the world, i chose to keep it
at wi(n)dow's length: an anchoress,
but with a maidservant to tend her.

another sign off

I JUST WANTED TO SAY *MEADOW* ONCE AND REALLY
  MEAN IT
TO SAY *(C)LOVER* ONCE AND MAYBE ONCE SAY *(S)UN*
  AND *(PL)UCK*
I JUST WANTED TO GO ON WITHOUT WHISPERING: *SOUL*
  SOUL SOUL
CAUSE, *SO WHAT SOUL, SO FUCKING WHAT?*

(I KNOW A LITTLE ANIMAL THAT IS ALL BODY
ALL *CHEEK* AND *FLEECE* AND *LUCK*)

aloft in a tangerine cloud

this morning, without warning, the house was lifted
by a fog it floated in the orange blue
of it the three layered cake of it
the windows blessings and paintings by some body
less body from a different from a diffident
century it was almost too beautiful
and that is difficult when you are naked or still
in your footed pajamas, the blue ones with the yellow
and red polka dots, or the smaller ones

in white we were
all there yet absent
this is how it will be light
light light years from now
when my children come to join me

in heaven, my god, look at me:
wreathed and blessed

the o antiphons

O Sweet Interrupt
O
O
O Sharpness, O Alacrity, O Lack

O Yeats O Browning O Keats

O Fellness of Purpose of Understanding
O Strange and Bitter Day after Day after Day
O Jocund Distillation
O Mother O Comfort
O Master O Litter O Rank

O Sweet Friend O Lyricist
O Plucker of these Few these Paltry Strings
O Sweet Pungent Smell you Drown your Small Room in
O Husband of Another
O Delighter in No Longer Me
O Betrayal
O Betrayer
OOO
Mine, Me.

o great slacker

because we are in love with Absence
because we can not love what we have see see Seen
because we need to believe in the Untenable, the Unbendable
because we know nothing can last last Last
because we have coined heard the absurd the term Everlasting
because We are Ever Last
because the last shall be first shall be the lost lost Lost
because we have read nothing from Start to Finish, from
    Refinish to Upstart
because we slowly learn, our Slowness Leaning
because our ambition is diluted by the Sweetness of holy Herb
    and Sleep
because our sleep melts in the Uprightness and the Uptightness
    of Drive
because when we Lack we Lack so proudly and so Well
because our thoughts need to spin on Something Else and
    Something Other, Something More
because we Spin and Toil and are nonetheless like the Lilies
like the poor poor lilies in the field field Field

becaUSE after a while Sorrow is a tasty Meat
beCAUSE we can't see ourselves Gnawing, Chewing
BEcause there is nothing New and nothing not New, Known
beCause we like to call ourselves WE and stand Together

beCaUse that allows ME to separate out from this sown this
   mown this cowering Crowd
and say onto you: i am your Remembrancer, your Requiter
i am Loud in your Sickness
you are Gnashing my Teeth
in Vain

this is the kind of poem i'm done writing, or,
a small pang in spring

She rose to His Requirements—dropt

down, down,
down.

she rose. she dropt.

do you, little tickbird, take . . .

do you
swallow?

do you, no-breasted wallow,
a small sparrow, you.

o, it was a pretty little field. in spots sown with eel grass.
in spots sown with dew.

hey, little seeker of truth.
hey lil' flower with the heavy heavy head.
the full and fulsome head

of the moon.

you don't look so good.

little sister, leave the husbandry to the husband.
or leave the husbandry.
(or leave the Husband.)

gave and took. like a rook.
gave and took.
head.

benighted but bedighted, I remain, yrs Love, O.
darkling, I listen.

when you stop dropping you start thinking.
when you start thinking you start.
. . . blinking.

darkling, I cheat.

here's where you say or do something (anything) honest.
here's where you present your true account.
(lest someone returning chide.)

anything?
honest?

here's where you resort to your old and tired (true and tested)
rhetorical devices. *(you would love the device.)*
(pang)

hey, loose and lanky.
hey, ephebe, did you mistakenly fall in love with a phoenix,
a philomel? a flicker? a fucking
Bird?

I am among the slaves.
I am slavish.
a scrannel pipe!

scrawny,
screwed, yrs . . .

hey, you, lover of truth, you don't
look so good.

ringstraked
and freaked, yrslove . . .

derailed and defunctive . . . and yrs and yrs and yrs . . .

I listened to everything everybody says.
(said, yeah yeah yeah, we heard . . .)

never got ahead.
never lost my head. I was losing my mind not losing my
head.

it tingles and it pricks, like nettles, like devil's club, like nasty
little
thoughts and rills.

scortatory, addicted
to borage and hellebore, yrs, love, O, look,
a small sorrow sown in with the sparrow grass!

husbandman and Wife.
lordandlover and other.
it didn't matter the end would be the same.
the lovage and the borage. the barrage.

turns out, I am the cock of the rock. gallinaceous and pug-
nacious and (pang): I guess,
a little disappointed.

like beckett in spring. ping.
like beckett in spring.

the garden of love

never had been,
never left

stripped from the waist up, love

and from the waist
down. low.

flankerbacked, love,
flatwise. slow.

flavesent,
and fleecy,
and fletched.

my flews, love.

i am not fleyed, love.
i flicker, love, but i do not
flinch.

flinders of my love, love.
flintlocked, flocked.

the floorage, love,
the floss.

flouting.
fluctuant.

here's my flue, love,
here's my fluff.

all the flummery, love.

i am flummox,
i am fluored,

love, i am flush.

flyaway, love,
fly-by-night
with your jibs and squirrels (and yes, your foxes and your
    fish).

the flyspeck-tacle of it! love,
the traps.

focalized, love,
thru the fogdog and the bank.

a mere foible, love,
and a moist foison, too.

folded, love,
yet quite foliate.

follow me, love,
for i am fond of you, love,

you are parsley and paradise.

i fool.
i foot.

it's in my mouth, love.

i have sent my footboy for you, love,

lambert, lambent. burnt.
o footle!

at a footpace,
at a footpace, love

all stalk and stall.

for you, love,
i forage, love, forasmush love
as is forbade, was forbore.

spy my forebearance, love,
eye my force, through ford and fore.

fore and aft love fore and aft.
cast brain bode.

it was foreordained, love
peak and paw.

shadow and shock, love
sight and skin.

mast and sail.

FOR there is LOVE, love,
and there is LOVED.

and there is More.

you are forgiven, love,
i will forgo, love, i will
go, love,
go.

if you are asked

Tell them

Your view has always been mullioned. Admit
Your own visions have always struck you
As useless, the way a photograph of spring can mean nothing
In spring. Refer to the books that have left you thumbmarked,
    open:
Or if you cannot remember their authors, simply show them
The thumbmarks, the indentations, that is, that are

Your temples. Mention you suspect the rest
Is merely ablation. Do not confuse them by speaking of the
    spite
Weeded out from the spikenard, of what the rosemallow does
Before it blooms. The saltmarshes, melting. The wired horizon.
Perhaps you should warn them:

This may not be for the faint of heart.

If you speak of the cloud
Of your unknowing, the longboat
Of your unknowing, the easychair
Of your unknowing, to them it will sound
Redundant.

Pace yourself.
Keep it short.

You do not want to risk disappearing in the middle
Of a sentence. Do not talk

Swedenborg, not even out in the garden,
Not even when you know what you are talking about: the
     burden
Made of burdock, the nettlesome heart. Why mention
The plow, the harrow, the tending to the empty? Remember,

To them you look just like a thirty-three(nine)-year-old woman.
You are a thirty-three(nine)-year-old woman, with or without

Your strange husbandry: the quiet apiary
Out back, the seed packets of fallow.
Do not get in that
Car. Admit that your life is still
Still and folded.

Show them the contact
Sheet. Do not

Mislead them by telling them your father died
Without troubling you. By not mentioning he never really
   wanted to be
That lucky. His rough-hewn hands.

You have already told them about your rose-strewn mother.

About the thin girl who lives across the street:
Tell them, you suspect some people actually inhabit
Their bodies. You, however, have suffered in a different

Way.

Do not call it suffering.

When asked about youth admit yours too was wasted.
When asked about beauty admit that you have been asking,
   too.
When asked about truth simply nod, yes.

You have already told them about your rose-strewn mother.

Try not to repeat yourself. When they ask you
About your influences

Be truthful, begin by mentioning
The weather: point to the lowlying clouds, or, if necessary,
The empty sky.

Then, but not angrily, quote them some Hopkins or just try to
Use the verbs: selves, faiths in a sentence

Out on a street that follows itself, a longing, in your pocket

A fraying photograph of spring and a list of words
You have always dreamt of.

You always knew you could not keep god's attention.

And it doesn't work, bulletproofing the heart.
The phenomenology of the soul, you have turned
And returned to it: the tending and the attending, the paying

With only your attention. Now, thin as a cloud,
You have carefully begun scraping out the inscape.
Tell them you fully intend to pitch it slowly
From without and within with pitch.

You have always wanted to be plainspoken.
You would have preferred to be misunderstood, tell them,

Like this.

forgoodisthelifeendingfitandfaithfully

a note on the author

Olena Kalytiak Davis "lives" in Anchorage, Alaska.

Poetry is vital to language and living. Since 1972, Copper Canyon Press has published extraordinary poetry from around the world to engage the imaginations and intellects of readers, writers, booksellers, librarians, teachers, students, and donors.

WE ARE GRATEFUL FOR THE MAJOR SUPPORT PROVIDED BY:

THE PAUL G. ALLEN
FAMILY FOUNDATION

Lannan

THE MAURER FAMILY
FOUNDATION

Anonymous

John Branch

Diana Broze

Beroz Ferrell & The Point, LLC

Janet and Les Cox

Mimi Gardner Gates

Gull Industries, Inc.
on behalf of William and Ruth True

Linda Gerrard and Walter Parsons

Mark Hamilton and Suzie Rapp

Carolyn and Robert Hedin

Steven Myron Holl

Lakeside Industries, Inc.
on behalf of Jeanne Marie Lee

Maureen Lee and Mark Busto

Brice Marden

Ellie Mathews and Carl Youngmann as
The North Press

H. Stewart Parker

Penny and Jerry Peabody

John Phillips and Anne O'Donnell

Joseph C. Roberts

Cynthia Lovelace Sears and Frank Buxton

The Seattle Foundation

Dan Waggoner

Charles and Barbara Wright

The dedicated interns and faithful volunteers of Copper Canyon Press

TO LEARN MORE ABOUT UNDERWRITING COPPER CANYON PRESS TITLES,
PLEASE CALL 360-385-4925 EXT. 103

The Chinese character for poetry is made up of two parts:
"word" and "temple." It also serves as pressmark for
Copper Canyon Press.

The poems are set in Palatino.
One of the most versatile and legible of all typefaces, Palatino
was created in 1950 by the prolific German type designer
Hermann Zapf. Named after the Renaissance calligrapher
Giambattista Palatino, this Old Face font is commonly used
for both text and display type. Palatino is so enduringly
popular that it is said to be the world's most heavily
pirated typeface design.

CPSIA information can be obtained
at www.ICGtesting.com
Printed in the USA
JSHW011737230123
36513JS00001B/3